Pathways to Artistry

A Method for Comprehensive Technical and Musical Development

Catherine Rollin

② TECHNIQUE

The goal of the *Pathways to Artistry* series is to emphasize the importance of technique and artistry beginning at the early stages of piano study. There are two books at each level of the series— *Technique* and *Repertoire.* Students can use them as soon as they have attained basic reading skills. The *Technique* books help students develop and understand the physical skills needed to play music artistically and with technical assurance. The *Repertoire* books bridge the gap between the early levels of method books and intermediate masterwork repertoire. Written to develop specific skills, the original music that I wrote for the *Repertoire* books will foster an appreciation for the sound and styles of masterworks while incorporating the physical vocabulary attained through the *Technique* books.

Good technique and musical artistry are inseparable. Their mastery is often a lifetime quest. It is my hope that through this series students will find themselves on the pathway to that goal.

Catherine Rollin

This book is dedicated to my students. As I have guided them on their individual pathways to artistry, I have discovered much about technique and music.

I would like to express my heartfelt appreciation to E. L. Lancaster for his input on the Pathways to Artistry Series. *He helped me organize and convey in print an approach to developing artistry that is central to my teaching. I would also like to thank my husband, Irwin Krinsky. His support and our ongoing dialogue about technique have helped me express my ideas with clarity and precision.*

Cover photo: Pierre-Yves Goavec/Getty Images

CONTENTS

HOW TO USE THE SERIES

The *Pathways to Artistry* Series can be used:

- **As a method:** Once students have acquired basic reading skills, *Pathways to Artistry Technique Book 1* and *Repertoire Book 1* can replace the instructional method book. Students can then continue with *Pathways to Artistry Technique Book 2* and *Repertoire Book 2*.

- **With a method:** *Pathways to Artistry Technique Books* and *Repertoire Books* can be used in conjunction with another method to reinforce reading skills and expose students to the sounds, technique, style, form and artistic ideas in the *Pathways to Artistry* series.

If students have not used this series as part of their early training, the *Technique Books* are recommended for transfer students at more advanced levels.

About *Pathways to Artistry* Technique Book 2

Technique Book 2 can be introduced as soon as students have completed *Technique Book 1* of this series. Although all of the technical skills from Book 1 are briefly reviewed, it is highly recommended that students go through Book 1 in its entirety before starting Book 2. The primary goals of the *Pathways to Artistry Series Technique Books* are to develop the physical skills needed to play artistically and to give students a physical vocabulary that will equip them to play the masterworks. Additionally, teachers and students find it easy to communicate when they have a shared vocabulary to clearly express the desired physical approach to the piano.

Technique Book 2 is divided into a prelude (review), six units and a coda (summary).

The **Prelude** reviews the Perfect Position at the Piano and the 12 Basic Skills from *Technique Book 1*.

Unit 1 introduces and explains four scale skills that are necessary to produce fluent and legato scale playing. These scale skills can be applied to many pieces in the piano repertoire.

Unit 2 introduces and explains six new technical skills that build on and add to the 12 basic skills introduced in *Technique Book 1*.

Unit 3 introduces the major scale pattern and uses it in the keys of C, G, D, A and E (Group 1 scales). This unit also explains chord inversions and the IV chord.

Unit 4 focuses on scale preparatory exercises for the Group 1 scales.

Unit 5 includes exercises using the six new technical skills.

Unit 6 features short etudes using the Group 1 scales and various other technical skills from *Technique Books 1* and *2*.

The Coda—The Coda summarizes the scale skills, new technical skills, scales, and chords presented in this book.

How to Use *Pathways to Artistry* Technique Book 2

Teachers should be familiar with the specific steps and vocabulary for each technical skill to effectively guide the initial presentation and review of the skills to the student. Teacher guidance is crucial to the student's understanding and execution of the skills. Students should proceed through the book systematically, following the order of presentation. Using Strong Fingers in all exercises is part of building a firm foundation. All exercises should first be practiced hands separately to master the physical skills presented.

The Three R's: Return, Review and Reinforce

Mastering technical skills is an ongoing process. The new skills presented in *Pathways to Artistry, Technique Book 2*, are used in all levels of music. Once students have gone through the entire book, they should **return** to **review** and **reinforce** skills as the need for them arises in their music.

PRELUDE–REVIEW

The Perfect Position at the Piano

A good pianist is a combination of musical artist and athlete. Like athletes who participate in sports and make "great plays," pianists must train and condition themselves to play greatly! Playing with good form is crucial to developing good technique.

Always be aware of the following elements of good form:

Posture

- Sit tall.
- Lean slightly forward from the hip.

Height

Sit at a height where:
- the shoulders are relaxed
- the forearms fall comfortably at a level with the keys
- the elbows can swing freely

Your feet should be firmly on the floor.

Distance

Sit far enough from the keyboard so that the arms have freedom.

Hand Position

- The thumb lies on its side.
- Fingers 2, 3, 4 and 5 fall in a natural curve. The fingers should maintain this natural curve as you play.
- Knuckles form a position that looks like a bridge.

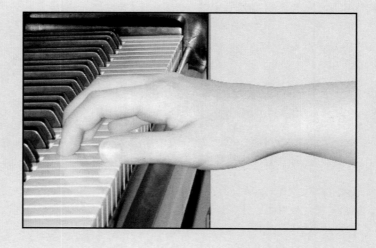

See Technique Book 1, pages 4–5, for additional information on The Perfect Position at the Piano.

The 12 Basic Technical Skills
(*Pathways to Artistry* Technique Book 1)

1. Elastic Wrist (page 6*)

   A. *Lift the wrist* to prepare.

   B. *Drop the wrist* with the weight of the arm.

   C. *Lift the wrist* and arm weight out.

2. Strong Fingers (page 7)

   A. *Curve the fingers*.

   B. *Play with the broad fingertip cushion, and with a little less than a 90° angle*.

   C. *Resist!*

3. Wrist Rotation (page 8)

   A. *Lift the wrist* to prepare, then *drop the wrist* with the weight of the arm.

   B. *Rotate the wrist*.

   C. *Lift the wrist* and arm weight out.

4. Two-Note Slurs (page 9)

   A. *Lift the wrist* to prepare.

   B. *Drop the wrist* with the weight of the arm.

   C. *Lift the wrist and arm weight out.*

5. Balancing Torso and Forearm (page 10)

   A. *Align.*

   B. *Lean.*

   C. *Follow.*

6. Finger Independence (page 11)

   A. *Hands separately.*

   B. *Hands together slowly.*

   C. *Be patient!*

7. Slurs (page 12)

   A. *Lift the wrist* to prepare, then *drop the wrist* with the weight of the arm.

   B. *Transfer the weight* from finger to finger.

   C. *Lift the wrist* and arm weight out.

8. Forearm Staccato (page 13)

   A. *Lift the hand* slightly off the keys.

   B. *Drop weight* with the hand and forearm as one unit, keeping the arm in motion.

   C. *Bounce* out.

9. Push-Off Staccato (page 14)

   A. *Lift the wrist* to prepare.

   B. *Drop the weight* of the arm into the playing fingers.

   C. *Lift the wrist* with a fast motion.

10. Rolling Wrist (page 16)

    A. *Lift the wrist* to prepare, then *drop the wrist* with the weight of the arm.

    B. *Lift the wrist* to start the circle.

    C. *Keep the wrist in motion (rolling).*

11. Arm-to-Arm Independence (page 17)

    A. *Hands separately.*

    B. *Hands together slowly.*

    C. *Be patient!*

12. Damper Pedal Technique (page 18)

    A. *Place* the ball of the foot on the damper pedal, heel firmly on the floor.

    B. *Depress* the foot and pedal as one unit.

    C. *Release* the pedal.

*The page numbers refer to *Pathways to Artistry* Technique Book 1.
See these pages for further explanation of the specific skills.

Unit One

Thumb Rolls (and hand shift)

Thumb rolls allow the entire hand to shift position either up or down while playing legato. They are necessary to create a true legato when crossing over in scales for the ascending left hand or the descending right hand. When crossing with fingers 3 or 4, the hand shift allows the fingers to cross as a unit.

Preparation before Playing

On a tabletop or the fallboard, place the right hand in the perfect hand position with the thumb relaxed on its side. Roll the tip of the thumb to the left so that the nail edge is now facing slightly downward. As you roll, the hand should simultaneously cross over the thumb and shift to realign. As the hand shifts, the second finger should fall directly to the left of the thumb. Roll back the thumb to the original position and simultaneously shift the hand to its original position. Repeat using the third finger and then the fourth finger to cross over. For third- and fourth-finger crossovers, the thumb will roll slightly more to the left. Repeat the entire exercise with the left hand—the thumb rolling to the right.

Three Steps for Developing Thumb Rolls:
A. **Roll the thumb** (to the left for the right hand or to the right for the left hand) so that the nail edge faces slightly *downward* toward the keyboard. (Roll more for crossovers of fingers 3 and 4.)
B. **Shift the hand to align** with the crossing finger or finger units as the thumb rolls.
C. **Return the thumb and hand** to their original relaxed position.

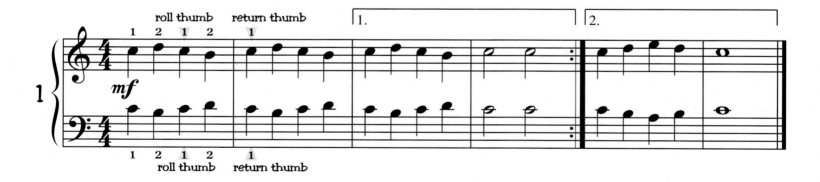

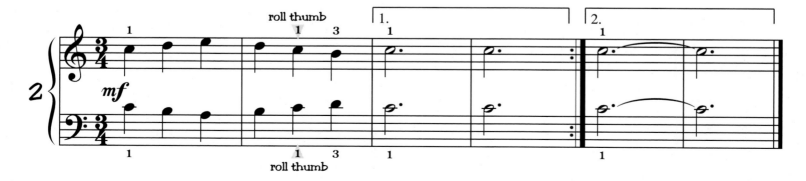

Repeat exercise 2 using finger 4 to cross over after the thumb roll.

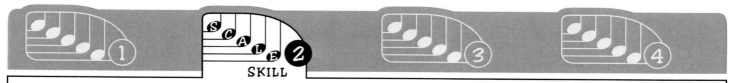

Thumb and Finger Pivots

Pivoting on the side of the thumb and on the fingertips allows the hand and arm to shift direction and transfers the arm weight into the playing fingers. These pivots are helpful for legato scale playing. In scale playing, thumb and finger pivots prepare the hand position for thumb-unders (see page 8) and realign the hand when the finger crosses after thumb rolls (see page 6).

Three Steps for Developing Thumb and Finger Pivots (Preparation for Thumb-Unders):

A. ***Keep the weight of the arm focused on the playing surface*** of the thumb or fingertip.

B. ***Turn or pivot*** gradually on the thumb and each finger preceding the thumb-under.

C. While pivoting, ***align*** the hand and arm smoothly with the pivoting thumb or finger.

Note: Exercise 1 is designed for the student to practice the pivot before actually passing the thumb under. This degree of pivot is only necessary when followed by a thumb-under. The arrows show the angle of the hand in relationship to the keyboard.

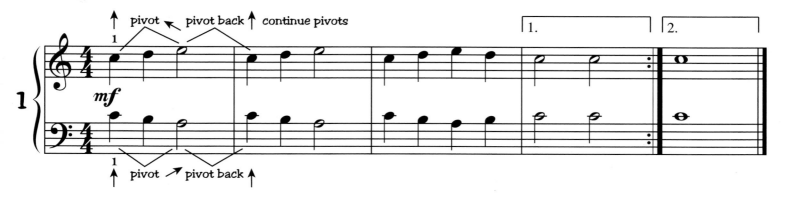

Three Steps for Developing Finger Pivots Followed by Thumb Rolls:

A. ***Keep the weight of the arm focused on the playing surface of the fingertip that crosses after the thumb roll.***

B. ***Turn or pivot*** on that surface.

C. ***Realign the hand*** as the crossing finger pivots. (The right hand will realign to the left. The left hand will realign to the right.)

Note: Exercise 2 is designed for the student to practice the pivot that takes place on the *one note* that follows the thumb roll. The arrows show the angle of the hand as it changes in relationship to the keyboard.

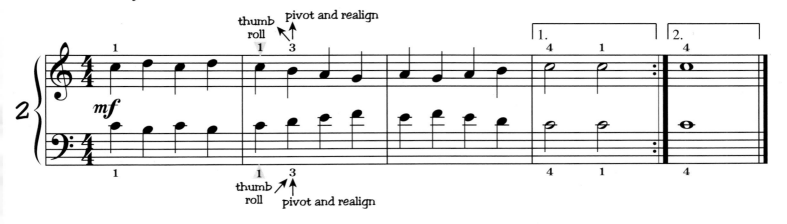

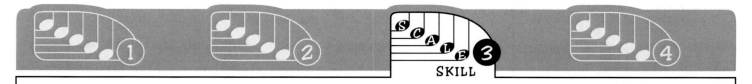

Thumb-Unders

Thumb-unders make more fingers available to continue playing a legato line ascending in the right hand or descending in the left hand.

Three Steps for Developing Thumb-Unders:

A. **_Pivot_** on the side of the thumb and the strong fingertip cushions, on the notes that precede the thumb-under.

B. **_Keep the pivoting fingers in motion_** while the **_thumb fluidly passes under._**

C. **_Realign_** the hand and arm with the thumb as it plays.

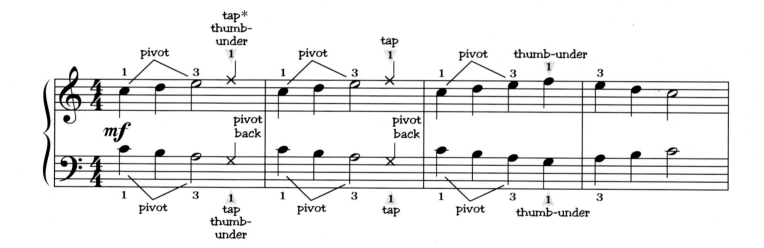

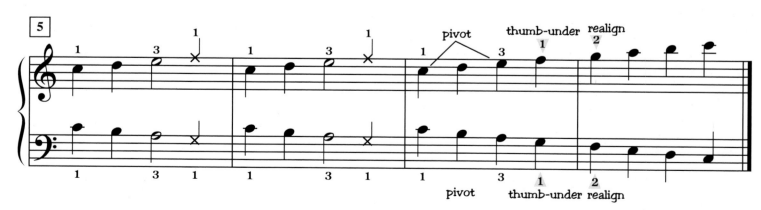

*Tap this key silently.

Legato Arm

The legato arm flows behind the playing fingers when playing scales. The elbow remains relaxed and smooth behind the forearm. The elbow or forearm should not be abruptly affected by the slight angle shifts of the hand during thumb and finger pivots, thumb-unders and thumb rolls.

Preparation before Playing

Place the right hand on the keys at the center of the keyboard. When either hand is at the center of the keyboard, the forearm is at a slight diagonal angle so that the elbow does not hug the body. The arm will then become more at a right angle to the keyboard when it is on high notes for the right hand and low notes for the left hand. Without depressing the keys, slide the hand up and down for approximately an octave, using a balanced torso and forearm. Repeat for two, three and four octaves. Keep the arm flowing fluidly behind the fingers and hand. Repeat with the left hand.

Three Steps for Developing a Legato Arm:

A. **Lift the wrist** to prepare, then **drop the wrist** with the weight of the arm.

B. **Form a slightly more diagonal line** to the keyboard to facilitate the thumb and finger pivots and thumb rolls.

C. **Keep the flowing arm uninterrupted** by the slight directional hand shifts during the thumb rolls, thumb and finger pivots and thumb-unders. The elbow should avoid abrupt movements.

Keep the legato arm moving fluidly while using the other scale skills on exercises 1 and 2.

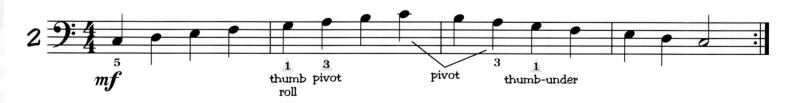

Using the Scale Skills

Use the legato arm on the following exercises.

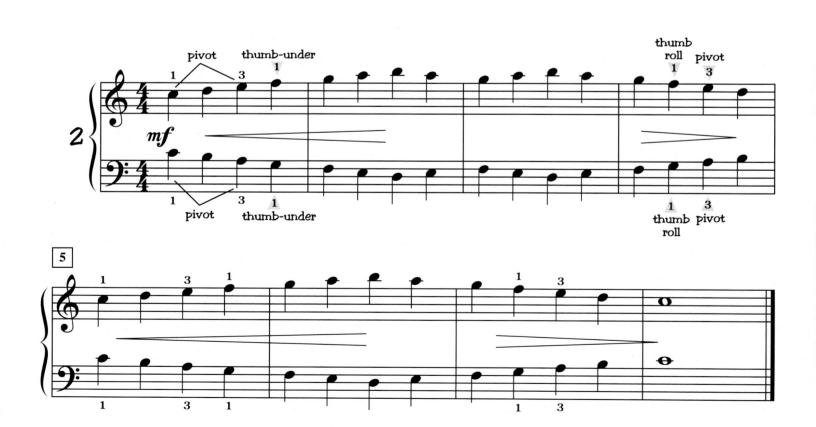

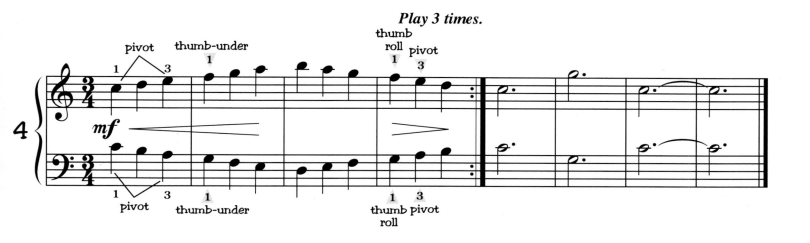

Unit Two

Overlapping Pedal

Overlapping pedal is used to create a seamless sound when a pedal change is indicated. Always use your ear as a guide for effective pedaling.

Three Steps for Developing Overlapping Pedal:

A. **Place and depress** the ball of your right foot on the damper (right) pedal. Keep the heel firmly on the floor.

B. **Lift the pedal simultaneously** with the key(s) being played at the pedal indication.

C. **Depress the pedal** immediately after the key(s) are played.

Preparation for Overlapping Pedal

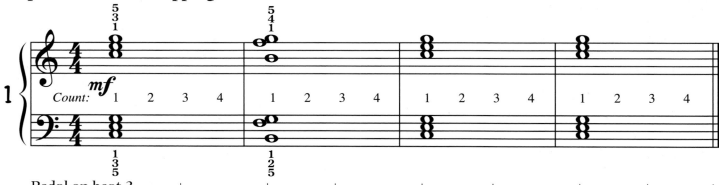

Pedal on beat 3.

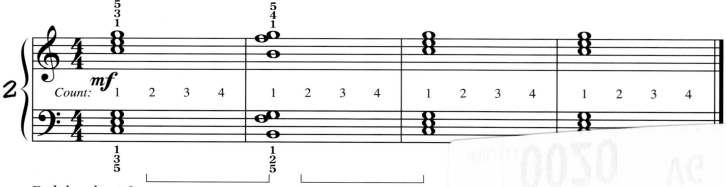

Pedal on beat 2.

Overlapping Pedal

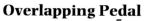

Pedal immediately after playing the chord on beat 1.

Under-Over Wrist Rolls

Under-over wrist rolls are used in repeated melodic patterns or as part of a melodic idea. Shifting the weight of the arm during the rising and falling of under-over wrist rolls gives melodies a musical shape and singing character.

Preparation before Playing

On a tabletop or the fallboard, place the weight of the right arm on the fingertip of the third finger. Using the fingertip as the axis of the circle, rotate the finger, hand, wrist and arm as one unit in a counterclockwise direction. As the circle begins, the wrist drops with the weight of the arm. As you rotate on the axis finger, place the opposite hand on the wrist to feel the *under-over* shape of the rotating hand. Repeat, using fingers 2, 4 and 5. Then repeat using fingers 2, 3, 4 and 5 of the left hand.

Three Steps for Developing Under-Over Wrist Rolls:

A. **Lift the wrist** slightly to prepare. **Drop the wrist and the weight of the arm** into the playing finger and simultaneously **begin a counterclockwise circle.** (The playing finger is the axis of the circle.) As the finger plays, the wrist drops into the *under* portion of the circle.

B. While **continuing the under motion** of the circle, **transfer the arm weight and align it** with the finger playing the highest key of each circular pattern.

C. **Lift the wrist** as the circle comes *over* the top. **(Return** to the original position and **keep the circle going** if the pattern continues.)

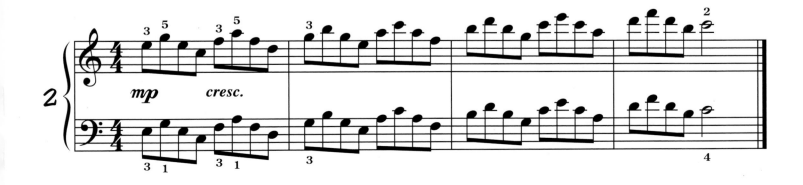

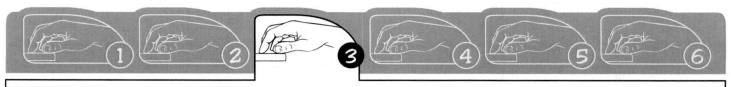

Portato

A portato has a slower release than typical staccatos. The sound created is a "sticky staccato." Portatos are helpful for many situations, including melodies that have a detached (but not very short) sound, repeated chord accompaniments, and full, resonant *fortes* on notes played with pedal.

Three Steps for Developing Portato Touch:
A. ***Lift the wrist*** to prepare.
B. ***Drop the wrist and the weight*** of the arm into the playing finger(s).
C. ***Lift the wrist*** and arm weight out with enough speed to ***release out*** of the keys for a detached (but not too short) sound. The slower the speed of the release, the longer the sound.

Use a portato with a faster release on all quarter notes for a more detached sound.

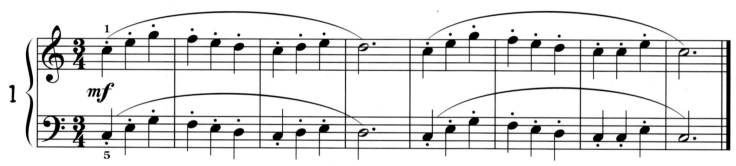

Use a portato with a slower release on all quarter notes for a less detached sound. Play this exercise 3 different times, each time releasing out of the keys more slowly to create "stickier" portatos.

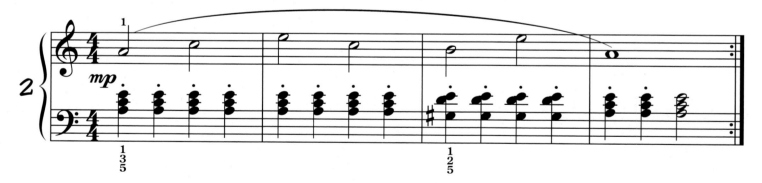

Use a portato with a medium speed release on all quarter notes for a resonant sound when played with pedal.

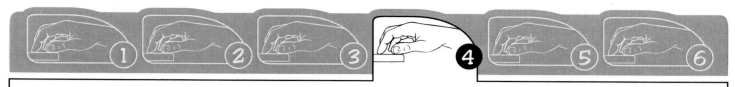

Wrist Staccato

Wrist staccatos produce a short, pointed sound. Wrist staccatos are often used for staccato melodies, as well as for fast repeated notes and chords.

Preparation before Playing

Rest your right hand on a tabletop or the fallboard. Keep the forearm stationary. The hand and fingers form one unit. Using the wrist as a hinge, tap the fingertips on the surface of the tabletop or fallboard. These taps, or little throws, out of the wrist hinge are like the motion used for dribbling a basketball and create a short, pointed-sounding staccato. The speed of the throw produces momentum that rebounds the hand back up to prepare for the next throw. You can gain momentum on the initial throw by lifting the hand and throwing faster. If you throw faster, you can get more than one tap (wrist staccato) from each throw. Try throwing once, but with more propulsion, resulting in two taps (wrist staccatos) as you throw the whole hand. Repeat and increase momentum, getting three taps (wrist staccatos) from one throw. (Think of throwing a ball one time, but getting multiple bounces from the one throw.) Repeat with the left hand.

Three Steps for Developing Wrist Staccato:

    A. ***Keep*** the forearm stationary.

    B. ***Lift*** the hand and fingers as a unit. ***Throw*** the playing fingers(s) into the key(s). This produces a short, pointed sound.

    C. ***Use*** the momentum of the throw to ***rebound*** for the next throw. (One fast impulse can produce multiple repeated staccatos.)

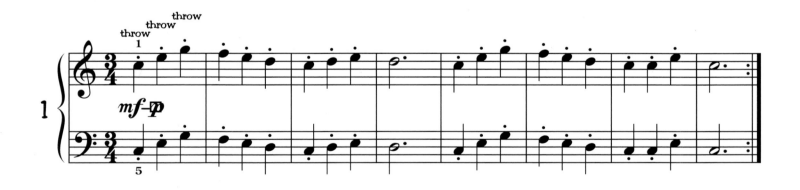

Trills

A trill is the alternation between two notes, usually an interval of a second. The trill consists of a minimum of four notes. It can start on the principal (written out) note or on the note above it, depending on the style period.

Preparation before Playing

When playing trills, it is important to gain momentum from the initial drop into the keys. This momentum enables the player to combine into one impulse the drop of the elastic wrist with wrist rotation. On a tabletop or the fallboard, play the exercise on this page using the following three steps for developing trills. Then play the exercise on the piano.

Three Steps for Developing Trills:

    A. ***Prepare and gain momentum for the impulse*** by lifting the weight out of the key(s). If the musical situation allows, lift slightly off the key surface.

    B. ***Combine dropping arm weight (elastic wrist) with wrist rotation*** on the alternating notes.

    C. ***Lift the wrist*** and arm weight out on the last note. (Steps B and C are propelled by impulse from the initial momentum of step A.)

    * Play the right hand two more times using these finger combinations: 3 1 3 and 2 1 2.
    Play the left hand two more times using these finger combinations: 1 3 1 and 1 2 1.

Voicing

Voicing focuses the weight of the hand on the melodic note. This enables the melody or main voice to project and sing above other notes that the same hand is playing.

Three Steps for Developing Voicing:

    A. First **play** only the melodic (voiced) notes. **Use** arm weight.

    B. **Add** the notes that are not voiced. Play these with a light, detached touch.

    C. **Continue** playing the melodic notes with heavier weight. **Play** the notes that are not voiced with less weight, but not detached.

After playing on the lap, play on the piano:

Unit Three   Major Scales, Triads and Inversions, Chords

Major Scales

The major scale consists of: whole step, whole step, half step, whole step, whole step, whole step, half step.

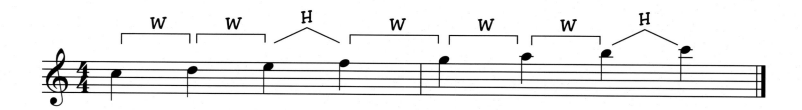

- When playing a scale, the scale skills of *thumb and finger pivots* and *thumb-unders* are used in the ascending right hand and the descending left hand.

- The scale skills of *thumb-rolls* and *finger pivots* are used on the descending right hand and the ascending left hand.

- The scale skill of *legato arm* is used ascending and descending in both hands.

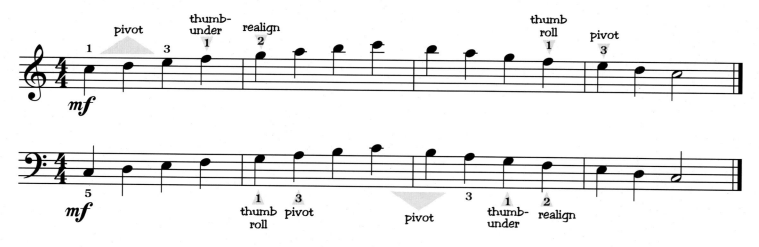

Group 1 Major Scales

All major scales have the same combination of whole and half steps. This pattern (W W H W W W H) can be played beginning on any key.

The scale fingerings are determined by the order of the white and black keys. The following five scales are part of the **Group 1** major scales because they all have the same fingering: **C, G, D, A** and **E.** Each new scale adds a sharp to the key signature to keep the same whole and half step pattern.

Play the Group 1 major scales hands separately only.

Optional: Transpose the exercises on pages 10–11 to the keys of G, D, A and E major.

Major Triads and Inversions

Major Triads

The major triad consists of two intervals of a third.
The bottom interval is a major third and consists of two whole steps.
The top interval is a minor third and consists of three half steps.

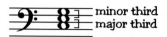

Inversions

There are three possible
positions for a triad:

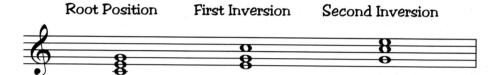

Play these root position triads and inversions.

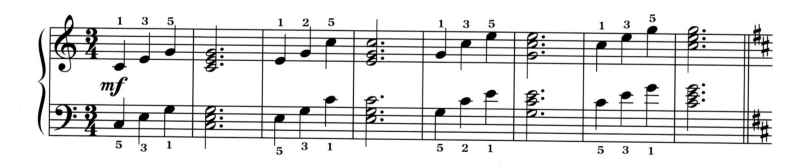

Continue with E, F, G, A, B and C major triads and inversions.

Chords

Reviewing the I and V⁷ Chord

The **I** chord is built on the first degree (note) of the scale, and consists of degrees 1, 3 and 5 of the scale.

The **V⁷** chord is built on the fifth degree of the scale, using the intervals of a 3rd, 5th and 7th above it. The **V⁷** chord often appears in first inversion, making it possible to move smoothly to the I chord. The 5th is usually omitted.

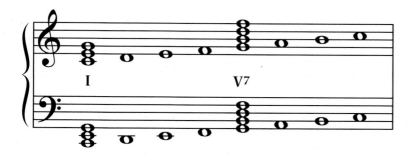

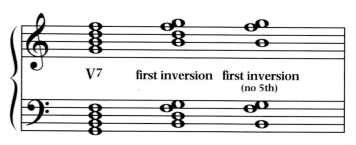

The IV Chord

The **IV** chord is built on the fourth degree of the scale, using the intervals of a 3rd and 5th above it.

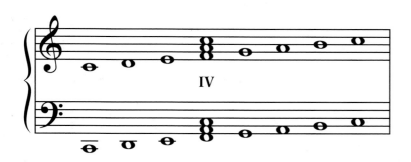

The IV Chord and its Inversions

The **IV** chord is used frequently in one of its inversions.

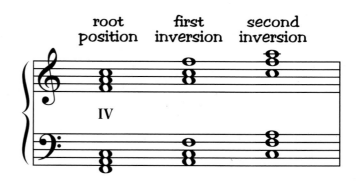

Primary Chords

The **I, IV,** and **V** (or **V⁷**) chords are known as the primary chords.

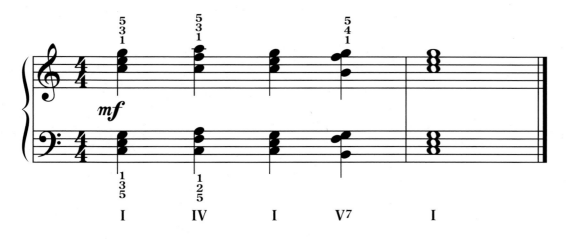

I–IV–I–V7–I Chord Progressions
Beginning on White Keys

Unit Four

C Major   All exercises use the legato arm.

1
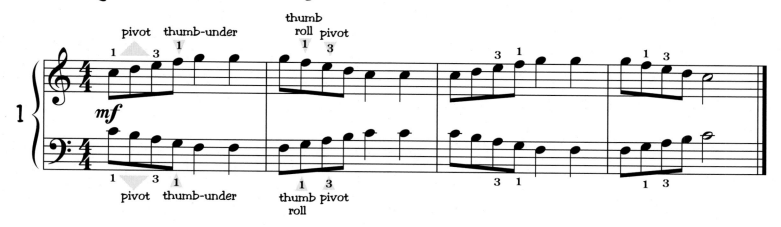

2
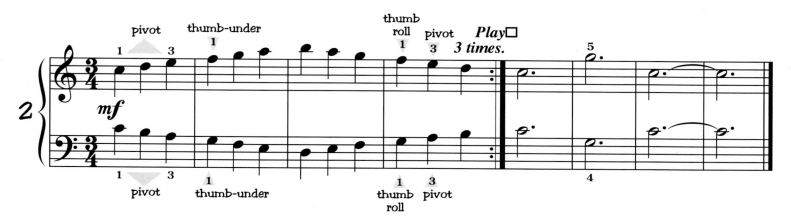

3
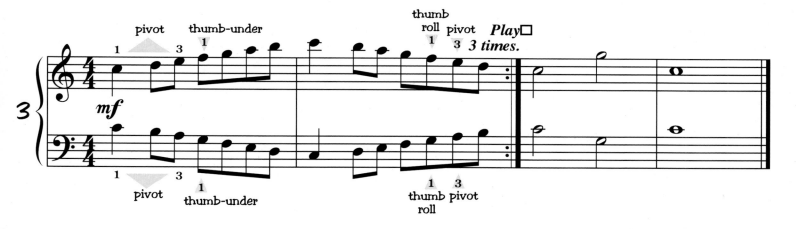

4
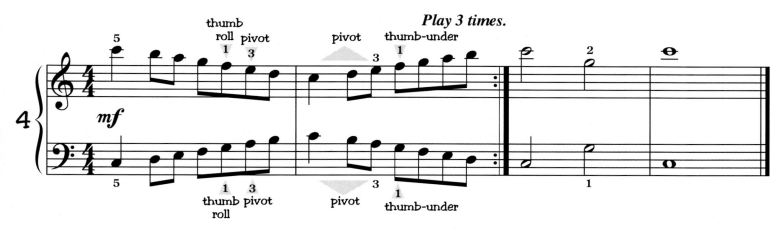

G Major   All exercises use the legato arm.

D Major   All exercises use the legato arm.

1

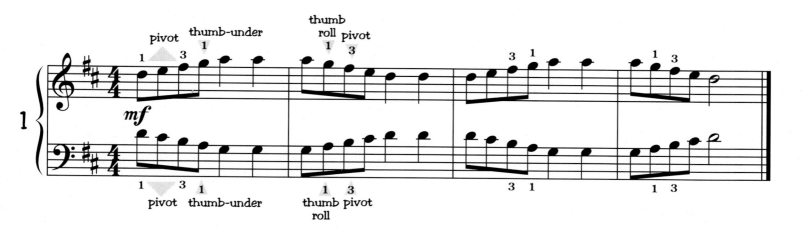

2

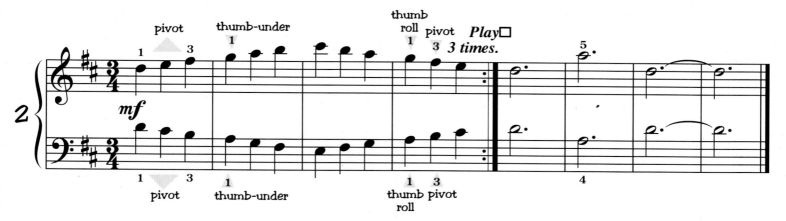

3

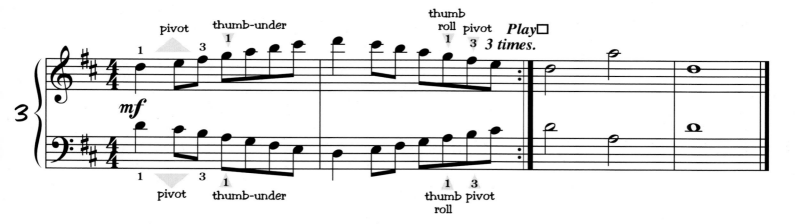

4

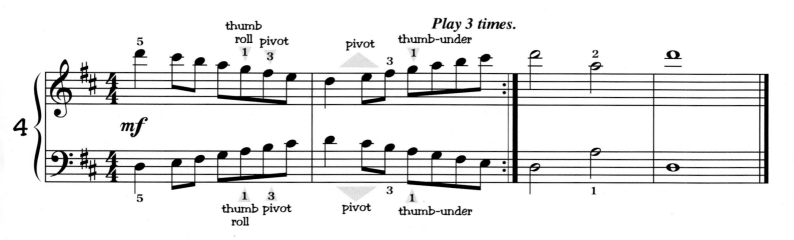

A Major   All exercises use the legato arm.

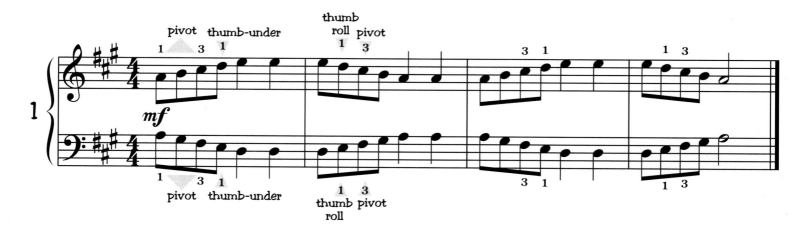

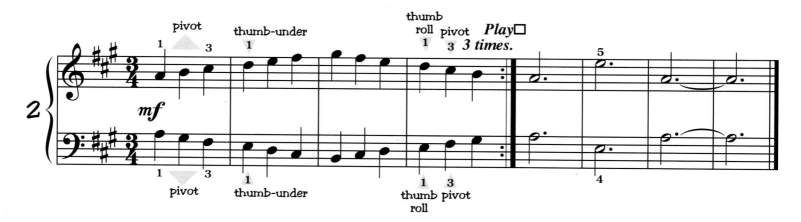

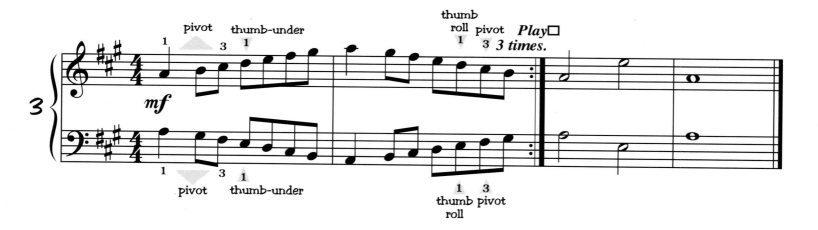

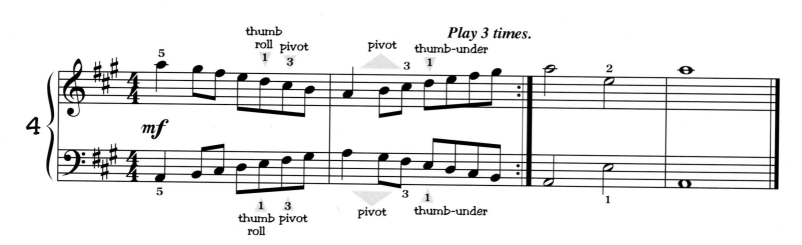

E Major All exercises use the legato arm.

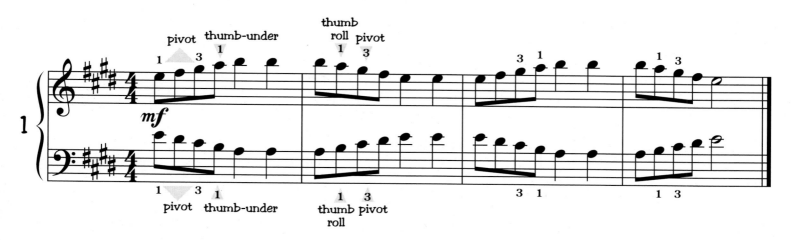

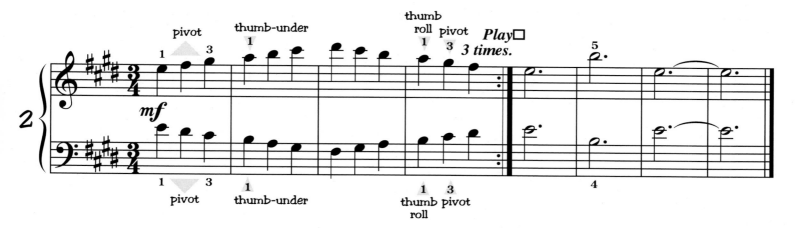

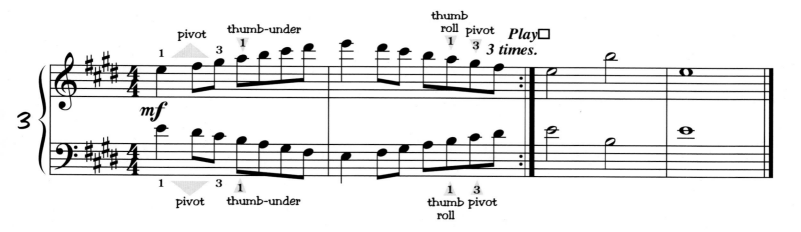

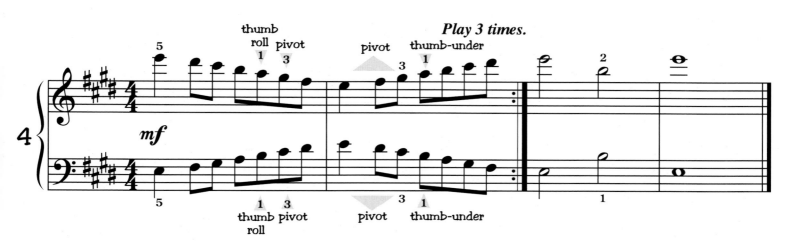

Unit Five

Using the Six New Technical Skills

1. Using Overlapping Pedal

> **Remember:**
> A. **Place and depress** the ball of the foot on the damper pedal, heel firmly on the floor.
> B. **Lift the pedal simultaneously** with the key(s) being played at the pedal indication.
> C. **Depress the pedal** immediately after the key(s) are played.

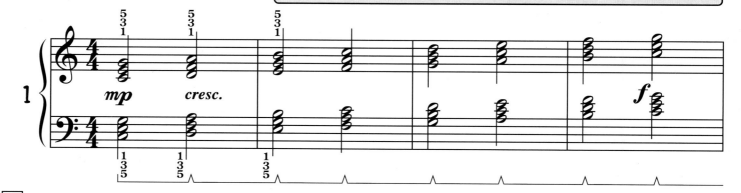

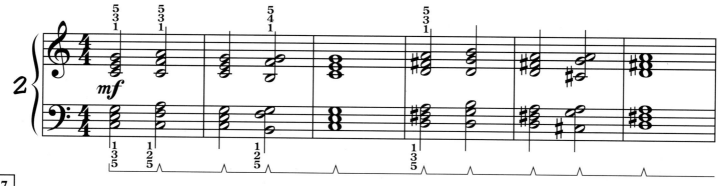

Continue with the keys of G, A, B and C major.

2. Using Under-Over Wrist Rolls

Remember:

A. *Lift the wrist* to prepare. ***Drop the wrist and the weight of the arm*** into the playing finger and simultaneously ***begin a counterclockwise circle.***

B. ***Transfer the arm weight and align it*** with the finger playing the highest key of each circular pattern.

C. *Lift the wrist* as the circle comes *over* the top.

Continue with E, F, G, A, B and C major patterns.

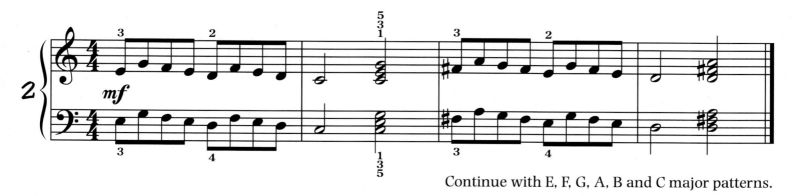

Continue with E, F, G, A, B and C major patterns.

Continue with E, F, G, A, B and C major patterns.

Continue with E, F, G, A, B and C major patterns.

3. Using Portato

> **Remember:**
> A. *Lift the wrist* to prepare.
> B. *Drop the wrist and the weight* of the arm into the playing finger(s).
> C. *Lift the wrist* with enough speed to *release out* of the keys for a detached (but not too short) sound.

Use a portato with a faster release on all quarter notes for a more detached sound.

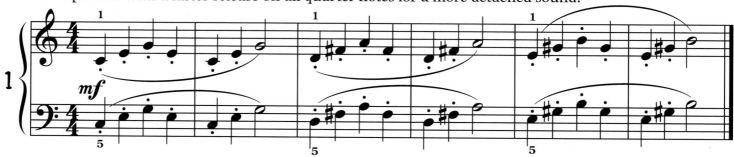

Continue with F, G, A, B and C major patterns.

Use a portato with a slower release on all quarter notes for a less detached sound.

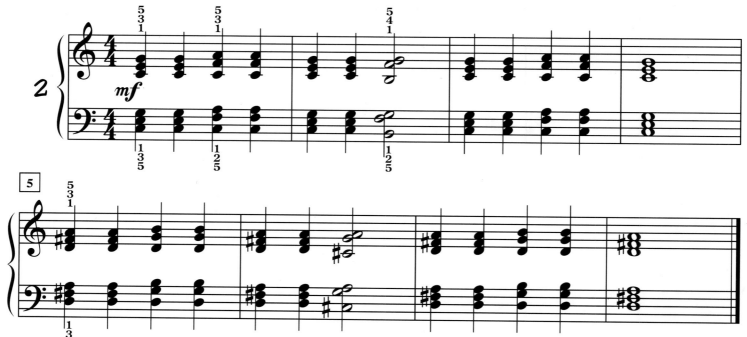

Continue in the keys of E, F, G, A, B and C major.

Use a portato with a medium speed release on all quarter notes for a resonant sound with pedal.

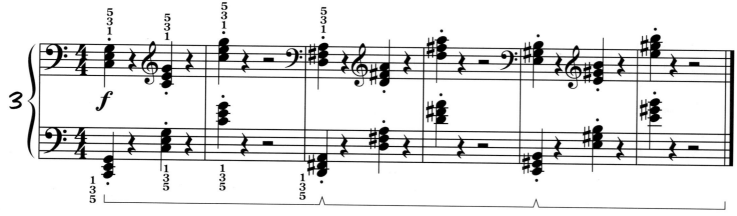

Continue with E, F, G, A, B and C major chords.

4. Using Wrist Staccato

Remember:

A. *Keep* the forearm stationary.

B. *Lift* the hand and fingers as a unit.
   Throw the playing finger(s) into the key(s).

C. *Use* the momentum of the throw to
   rebound for the next throw.

Continue with E, F, G, A, B and C major patterns.

Continue with E, F, G, A, B and C major patterns.

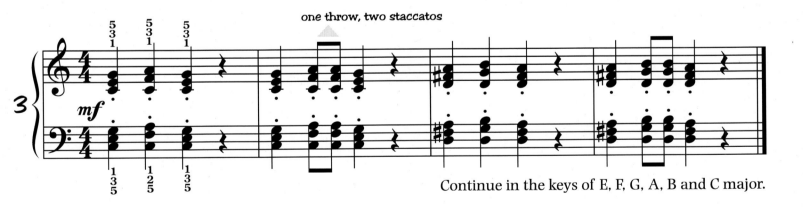

Continue in the keys of E, F, G, A, B and C major.

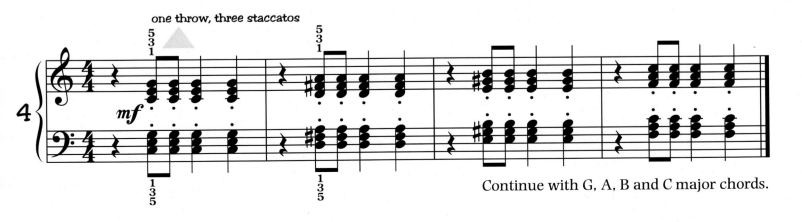

Continue with G, A, B and C major chords.

5. Using Trills

> **Remember:**
> A. *Prepare and gain momentum for the impulse* by lifting the weight out of the key.
> B. *Combine dropping arm weight with wrist rotation.*
> C. *Lift the wrist* and arm weight out.

Play the right hand two more times using these finger combinations: 3 1 3 and 2 1 2.

Play the left hand two more times using these finger combinations: 1 3 1 and 1 2 1.

6. Using Voicing

Remember:

A. First **play only** the melodic notes. **Use** arm weight.

B. **Add** the notes that are not voiced (non-melodic). **Play** these with a light, detached touch.

C. **Continue playing** the melodic notes with heavier weight. **Play** the notes that are not voiced with less weight, but not detached.

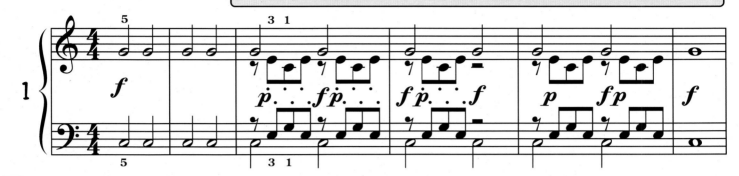

Continue with E, F, G, A, B and C major patterns.

Continue No. 2 and No. 3 with D, E, F, G, A, B and C major patterns.

* In exercises 2 and 3, play the notes with downstems in measures 6–7 with a light, detached touch.
 In measures 10–11, play the notes with downstems lightly, but not detached.

Unit Six

C Major

Preparation: Play the C major scale and primary chords hands separately.

*Etudes are pieces that focus on technical skill.

G Major

Preparation: Play the G major scale and primary chords hands separately.

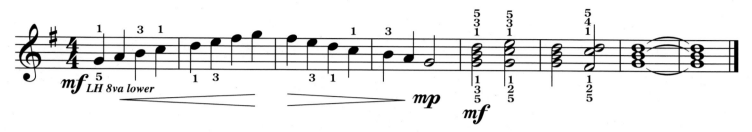

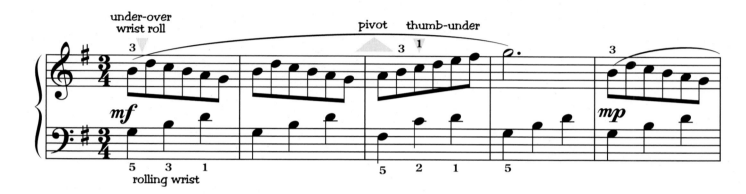

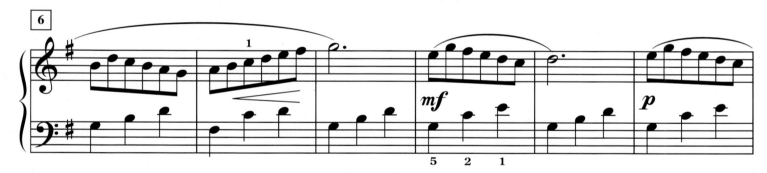

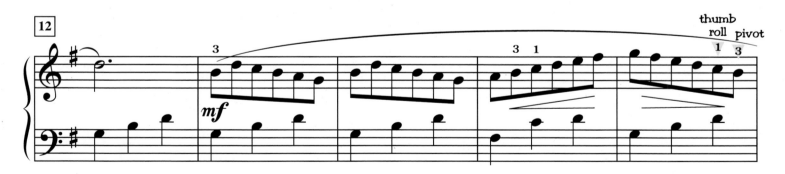

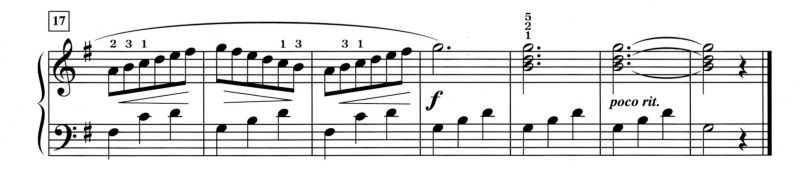

D Major

Preparation: Play the D major scale and primary chords hands separately.

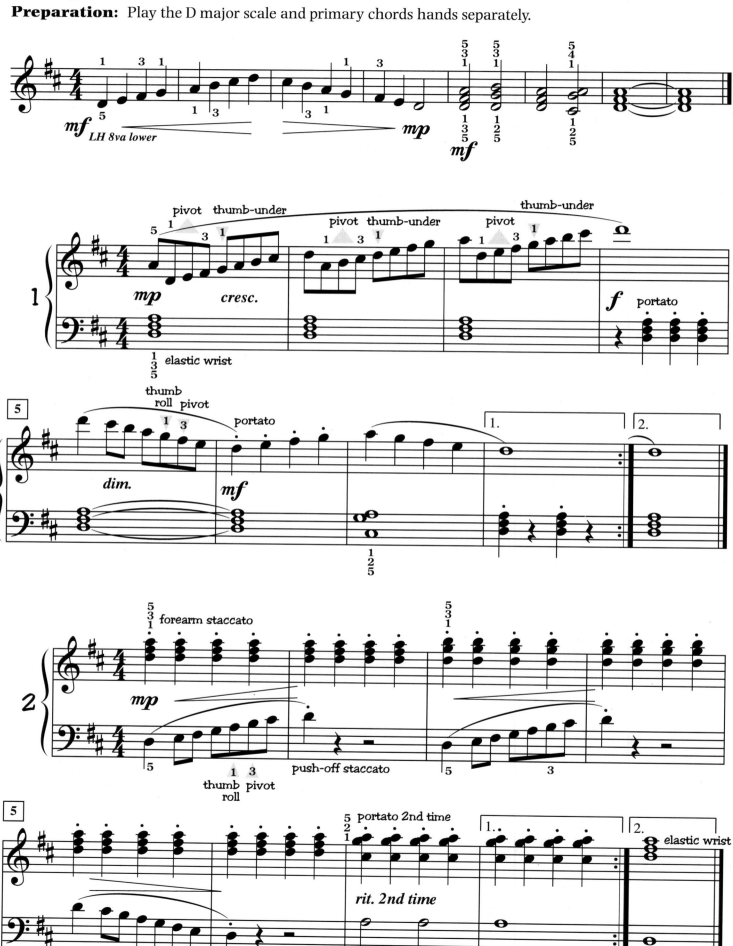

A Major

Preparation: Play the A major scale and primary chords hands separately.

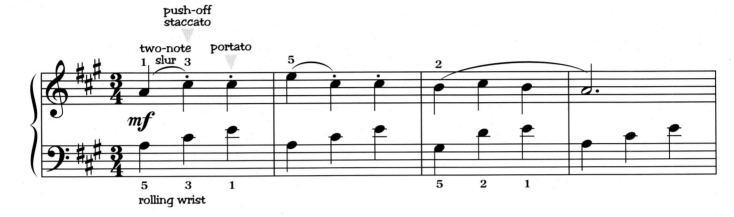

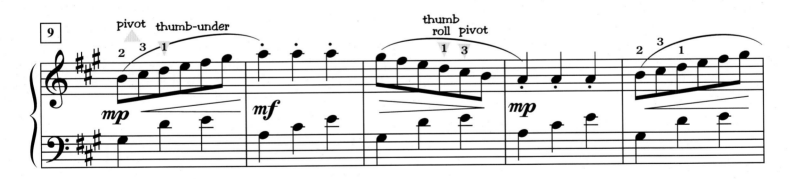

E Major

Preparation: Play the E major scale and primary chords hands separately.

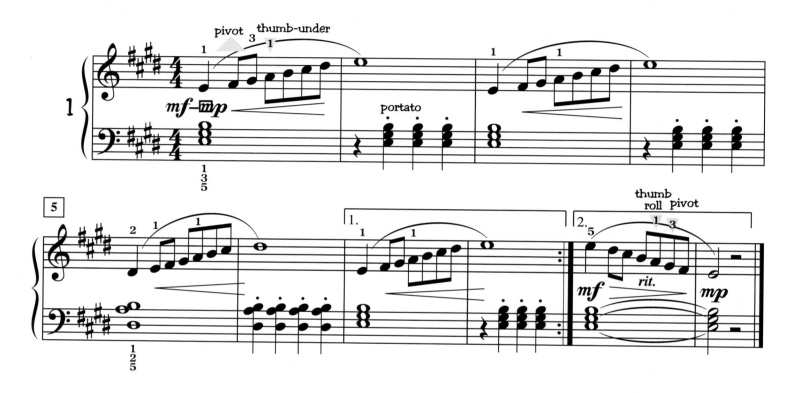

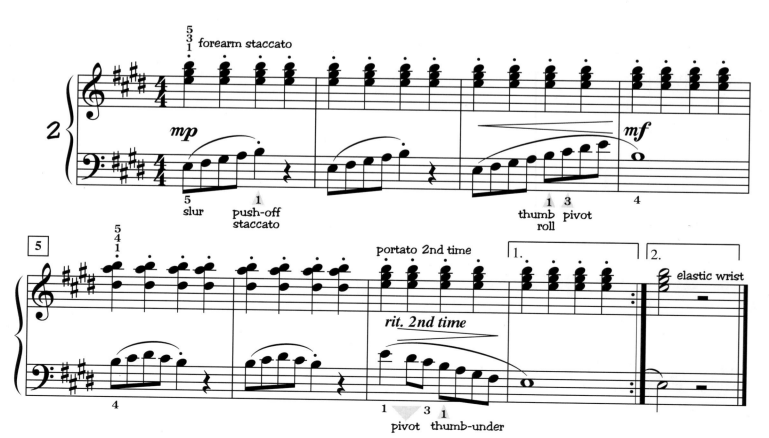

Technical Index

Coda

Scale Skills

1. **Thumb Rolls (page 6)**

   A. ***Roll the thumb downward*** toward the key.

   B. ***Shift the hand to align*** with the crossing finger or finger units as the thumb rolls.

   C. ***Return the thumb and hand*** to their original position.

2. **Thumb and Finger Pivots (page 7)**

   A. ***Keep the weight of the arm focused on the playing surface of the thumb or fingertip.***

   B. ***Turn or pivot on that playing surface.***

   C. ***Align or Realign: Align*** the hand and arm with the playing thumb and fingers as they pivot (in preparation for thumb-unders). ***Realign*** the hand as the crossing finger pivots (after thumb rolls).

3. **Thumb-Unders (page 8)**

   A. ***Pivot*** on the side of the thumb and the strong fingertip cushions, on the notes that precede the thumb-under.

   B. ***Keep the pivoting fingers in motion*** while the ***thumb fluidly passes under.***

   C. ***Realign*** the hand and arm with the thumb as it plays.

4. **Legato Arm (page 9)**

   A. ***Lift the wrist*** to prepare, then ***drop the wrist*** with the weight of the arm.

   B. ***Form a slightly more diagonal line*** to the keyboard to facilitate the thumb and finger pivots and thumb rolls.

   C. ***Keep the flowing arm uninterrupted*** by the slight directional hand shifts during thumb and finger pivots, thumb rolls and thumb-unders. Avoid all abrupt movement of the elbow.

Six New Technical Skills

1. **Overlapping Pedal (page 12)**

   A. ***Place and depress*** the ball of the foot on the damper pedal, heel firmly on the floor.

   B. ***Lift the pedal simultaneously*** with the key(s) being played at the pedal indication.

   C. ***Depress the pedal*** immediately after the key(s) are played.

2. **Under-Over Wrist Rolls (page 13)**

   A. ***Lift the wrist*** to prepare. ***Drop the wrist and the weight of the arm*** into the playing finger and simultaneously ***begin a counterclockwise circle.***

   B. ***Transfer the arm weight and align it*** with the finger playing the highest key of each circular pattern.

   C. ***Lift the wrist*** as the circle comes *over* the top.

3. **Portato (page 14)**

   A. ***Lift the wrist*** to prepare.

   B. ***Drop the wrist and the weight*** of the arm into the playing finger(s).

   C. ***Lift the wrist*** with enough speed to ***release out*** of the keys for a detached (but not too short) sound.

4. **Wrist Staccato (page 15)**

   A. ***Keep*** the forearm stationary.

   B. ***Lift*** the hand and fingers as a unit. ***Throw*** the playing finger(s) into the key(s).

   C. ***Use*** the momentum of the throw to ***rebound*** for the next throw.

5. **Trill (page 16)**

   A. ***Prepare and gain momentum for the impulse*** by lifting the weight out of the key.

   B. ***Combine dropping arm weight with wrist rotation.***

   C. ***Lift the wrist*** and arm weight out.

6. **Voicing (page 17)**

   A. First ***play only*** the melodic notes. ***Use*** arm weight.

   B. ***Add*** the notes that are not voiced (non-melodic). ***Play*** these with a light, detached touch.

   C. ***Continue playing*** the melodic notes with heavier weight. ***Play*** the notes that are not voiced with less weight, but not detached.

Major Scales, Triads and Inversions, Chords

Major Scale

Whole step, whole step, half step, whole step, whole step, whole step, half step

Major Triads and Inversions

Major Triads

A major triad in its root position is built from bottom to top, with a major third on the bottom (two whole steps) and a minor third on the top (three half steps).

Inversions

There are three possible positions for a triad:

Root Position

First Inversion

Second Inversion

Primary Chords: I, IV and V (or V7)

I Chord

A chord built on the first degree of the scale (notes 1, 3 and 5 of the scale).

IV Chord

A chord built on the fourth degree of the scale, using the intervals of a 3rd and 5th above it. It is often played in the second inversion when it follows the I chord in root position.

V7 Chord

A chord built on the fifth degree of the scale, using the intervals of a 3rd, 5th and 7th above it. It is often played in first inversion and simplified to a three-note chord.